I0191427

THE LIGHTHOUSE

Be your own Guardian Angel

ARCHANA UPADHYAY

/ BookLeaf
Publishing
India | USA | UK

Made with ❤ on the BookLeaf Publishing Platform
www.bookleafpub.in
www.bookleafpub.com

Dedication

To all those beautiful people who made me learn, evolve
and be a better being.

To my dear Mom, my first guru.

To my Dad, for empowering me.

To my Husband, who is positivity personified.

To my Angel Daughter, who believes in me and
motivates me to steer ahead.

To my Friends who stand like a rock for me.

To my Students who make me connect and feel the pulse
of the new generation.

To my CRITICS who make my resolve stronger and
stronger.

And, to my Readers, who after reading this book will
join the march to self-discovery.

Preface

Everyone gets one life to live.
Why complicate it?

Look within.
You are:
The Healer, the Counsellor, the Powerhouse, the
Lighthouse
Unleash, unfetter, unbar
Curate, chisel, create.
It's your life!
The poet wants you to read, feel, evolve and inspire.

Acknowledgements

I thank the Supreme being, the universe, and the infinite
wisdom that directs me.
I see the lighthouse in me, steady and bright through the
turmoil and peace of life.
Thankful for the trials and victories, the highs and lows
which mold me.
Thank you for the gift of life, for the air that fills our
lungs, and for the heart that beats with love and purpose.
I bow to the divine within, the spark that lights my soul
and lights my way.

1. The Bridge

The Bridge hangs sturdy, joined with strings,
Over the river with inherent mood swings,
From serenity to an outrageous uproar.
Unfazed, it lets million steps march across,
Safely, even when the river is crass and cross.

Build a bridge between the self and the world outside.
It will subdue the untamed, tumultuous rising tides.
Traverse through it with the faith within.
Be deaf to taunts and listen to the echoes of your soul.
Applaud your journey, to reach your goal.

2. A Rain Drop Bids Adieu

A raindrop embarked on its journey,
From the portals of the skies.
Uninterrupted, it was a free fall.
Unsure of its halt.

Sadness engulfed its rapidity
For soon it would lose its entity.
Worried, where she would fall?

On a bed of flowers?
Or a patch of green?
Into an expanse of ocean?
Or on dwellings or creatures?

Closer to the earth
It felt a mirth.
It's not a fall.
But a journey to bless
some, if not all.

It slid on the blade of grass.
And melted into the soil,
To moisten the seed, in the earth's womb.

It breathed in the seed.
It lived in the plant.
O, What a mighty fall!

3. Earth Unmuted

Giving space to my neighbours, on my axis I glide,
To let life bask in the care I provide.
Neither too fast, nor too slow.
Not rushing, just a placid flow.

I always have enough for all creatures and creeds.
Then O human! Why this greed?
I have room for the tiniest to the mammoth race.
Then why encroach on others space?

Your hands and mind are destined for creation.
Then why are they busy in meaningless destruction?
Why this cold, ignorant apathy?
For the creatures put at your mercy.

The greasy, venomous black rivers, lakes and lagoons.
The skies overcast with toxic, cancerous fumes.
The tonsured surface dotted with dust and grime.
The reckless plunder of my wealth, the bleeding mines.

Oh, the extinct beings, courtesy your habit to trespass.
The wailings of fellow creatures tormented and aghast.
Look, what you have done in the name of civilization.

Hold! Is annihilation your destination?

Will you ponder over your misdeeds?
And atone for the havoc you unleashed?
I am life, I love creatures pulsating with activity, so
splendid.
Locking the life and putting you down, I never intended.

Now promise, tomorrow when you swing back to life.
Do not suck life out of your own planet.
Breathe, do not pant.
Walk, do not rush.
Harness, but not exploit.
Go for creation, not madless production.

There is enough till posterity.
Why vainly veering towards vanity?
Log in to life. Unlearn. Undo. Unwind.
I once again nominate you as my caretaker, O mankind!

4. The Orchestra

The orchestra fascinates me.
An ensemble of countless musicians,
Each with a different voice,
Yet together, they breathe harmony.
The violin, the guitar, the drum,
Melt into one seamless soul.

What births this magical blend?
Is it talent? The focus of each hand?
Or the Conductor, who lifts them,
Above the rants and cheers of the world,
Guiding them to dwell
In scales, notes, and rhythmic spell?

My life, too, unfolds like an orchestra.
Why can't I be the conductor of my own show?
Let me strum the strings of challenge,
Tap the drums of defiance,
And compose a melody called life,
A symphony of courage, grace, and no strife.

5. The Name

What is a NAME?
An identity, a tag, a label?
It's mine yet chosen by others.
Picked with care, meaning, and trend,
Then softened into a pet name,
Simple, quirky, easy to call.

Then come the labels,
Shaped by moods, traits, and tempers.
Some to show love,
Some to remind you, you're the black sheep.
Friends add theirs,
To tease, to mock, or just for fun

Others too feel their birth right to call you names,
When you don't meet their expectations.
A gallery of names,
Each echoing a moment, a mood.
Are you Confused? Baffled?
Don't be.

Turn a deaf ear to the noise.
Choose the word that defines you.

This is your life, your story unfolding.
Be the author.
Script each chapter
In your own voice.

6. Two Leaves and the Rain

As I hailed a cab and settled in tight,
The skies unleashed a torrent, a sudden delight.
Thankful to be dry, I watched through the pane,
Leaves dancing in rain, trees bathed in joyous refrain.

The cab crawled, horns blaring, in traffic's snare,
But outside, nature reveled without a care.
Dogs hid in alcoves, birds sang from above,
No complaints, just acceptance, a lesson to love.

A whispered secret caught my curious ear,
A leaf of bougainvillea spoke, without fear.
'We leaves rejoice, our thirsty souls revive,
While humans fret, under shelters, they strive.'

A wild leaf nodded, said, swaying gently in the breeze,
'Let's cherish present joys, in life's fleeting ease.
In chasing grand dreams, don't miss small delight,
Cherish every moment, bless your day and night.

7. Pills to My Ills?

Why do I crib?
Why do I sulk?
Why do I complain?
IS IT BECAUSE
Things do not happen my way.
People don't act my way.
Someone doing better than me?
Have I set goals more than I can achieve?
Am I carrying the burden of my parents' dreams?
HALT! THINK!
Sulking, complaining, cribbing
ARE THEY Pills to my ills?.
NO!
They close my door to have a better perspective to my problem.
They blind me to see problems as opportunity.
Let me open my door to shunt them out.
And let the breeze with new outlook come in.

8. Punctuations

My teacher never paused, when she talked about the value of full stop,
While we waited for it eagerly when the talk would become quite long.
We would exclaim with sorrow when we got a minus 2 in the papers,
Because we had forgotten to put those silly symbols in our answers.

Once I almost slipped into coma when my teacher cut 5 marks in an absurd way
As I did not put those silly tail-like structures, the commas while writing my essay.
A big question mark haunted me for this marking, unfair and gory,
But consoled myself and felt it was better to put a full stop to this sob story.

The hyphen provided no high fun because I felt it was trespasser into the language,
A trouble monger for students, apathetic to our feelings with no intention to salvage.
Well, I do not want to dot my feelings with dot family,

but deciphering them was indeed a trauma,
The two dots one above the other and its irritating sister,
a dot above the comma.

Do you know the ordeal one goes through like a maze,
When you have to hunt for them while typing a
message.
One wrong symbol brought such a misunderstanding
with my friend.
It brought out long but not lasting friendship to an
ignoble end.

If you believe in poetic justice, then look at the irony of
my fate,
I became a language teacher, so these symbols I could no
longer hate.
And now I had to give them a royal treatment,
Gradually, I realised their value with fair assessment.

When you speak, you vary your tone and modulate,
Inflecting emotions, a heartfelt way to intonate.
Your words convey meaning, lucid and clear,
A symphony of feelings, for the world to hear

Symbols are emissaries of the life,

O how they made me realise,

To pause intermittently my maddening race against time.

To make life enjoyable and sublime.

9. Two Wheels

Two wheels of a bicycle, once joined, a perfect pair,
Years of harmony, without a single care.
But unity broke, and they went their way,
Each feeling wronged, in their own say.

The rear wheel said, 'The front's a tyrant true,
Dictating terms, with an air so rude.
The front wheel retorted, 'You're lazy and slow,
Always lagging behind, don't you know?'

Their once-smooth ride, now a discordant sound,
As they moved apart, their bond unbound.
No longer in sync, their paths did stray,
A reflection of relationships gone astray.

Yet, in their hearts, a glimmer remains,
Of the joy they shared, the miles they gained.
So, the new journey began on individual paths,
Moving in opposite directions, energy lost in wrath.

The conflict sustained for days,
Egos stood tall, in stubborn ways.
No movement, no action, just sordid reaction,
Days passed, and egos slowly lost their inflation.

Realisation dawned, and egos deflated,
A smile at each other, harmony created.
The paddles moved forward, in sync they steered,
Weaving threads of inner symphony, love appeared.

10. Zero Balance

How can they pay if their bank shows zero balance.
Have pity on them and exonerate them.
They could only deposit comments; sarcastic, ironic,
scathing and piercing.
The more they withdraw, the more they deposit.
For they derived sadistic pleasure from this transaction.

They could never deposit complements, praise and
admiration.
How could they ever spend these precious currencies of
enormous denominations.
Have pity on morally bankrupt bankers of life.
Lend them some values and virtues from your own vault,
The lender and the borrower, both earn profit, by default.

11. The ETIQUETTE

Uncle greets the elders very humbly,
He exchanges pleasantries with neighbours so nobly,
He even opens the car doors for ladies so gently.
He is called a gentleman so fondly.

My dad tells me to imbibe manners like him.
My mom tells me to be humble and polite like him.
My grandpa wants me to have etiquette like him.
My teacher wants me to be honourable like him.

Yesterday, I saw him arguing with a vegetable vendor.
And he used impolite words for the street sweeper.
He just threw the money at the rickshaw puller.
He thew the plate at aunt as his mood was bitter.

I don't want to be like him.
I will be myself: the same with one and all.

12. Hunt the Hunters

The dogs bark noisily,
The asses bray loudly,
Everyone blows one's own trumpet.
To sound, not better but louder than others.

This is how people exist, to compete and out do others.
If they can't beat your talent, they hunt your confidence.
If they can't match up with you, they dent into your
personality.
They find faults with you and break you into pieces.

You have only one shield against these attacks.
Your core strength and confidence.
You are as enormous as the Universe.
Hunt the trespassers out of the territory of your inner
cosmos.
This life is your land, till it, and grow the plants of your
choice.

For every shadow seeks to diminish the shimmer.
Stand tall like ancient oaks, roots deep in resolve,
Brush off the whispers of doubt that scorn your worth.
Nurture what brings you joy, allow it to evolve,

Let the dogs bark noisily,
Let the asses bray loudly,
You play your own music and march stoutly.

13. Know Thyself!

You are a treasure trove of courage, know thyself,
The Abhimanyu within, who can break free from the
wheel's spell.
You are Karna, unbound by doubt or fear,
No Shalya's words can pierce your armor, your
confidence clear.

You are Sita, steadfast and strong,
Upholding dignity, righting the wrong.
You are Eklavya, skilled and wise,
Your inner wealth surpasses external prize.

You are Chanakya, strategic and bold,
Toppling tyranny, your wisdom engraved in gold.
You are Hanuman, loyal and true,
Tapping inner power, to see you through.

Why forget your strength, your inner might?
Rise up, shine forth, let your spirit take flight.
You have the power to overcome the great,
To conquer challenges, to seal your fate.

14. A Pair of Slippers

We enter barefoot.
And exit barefoot.
But between the entry and the exit,
Life walks on a pair of slippers.

Existing beneath the feet,
But above the surface,
Bearing the weight,
Protecting all ages.

Walking up to the temple gate,
But lying outside in long wait.
Taking us to the cot so we rest for a while.
But kept like an outcast on the floor tile.

From stylish to the simplest,
From perfect, to the shabbiest,
For the pedicured feet,
To feet with freckled heels.

Bad omen if one on other.
Good omen to hang a broken piece.
A weapon to vent out angst.
Made into a garland to humiliate.

Bathed, flung, discarded.
Mended, stolen, taken for granted.
Uninfluenced by caste colour or creed,
Immune to any favours or greed.

I comfort all fair and square,
Value or devalue me, O wise creatures,
I am happy to be a pair of slippers

15. The Curry Leaves

Light green bunch of sparkling leaves,
An ordinary presence amidst a melee of exotic greens.
Yet see the magic of leaves crackled in oil,
The aroma wafts out casting a nourishing spell.

In my balcony, the curry plant, once lied in an earthen
pot.
A dead stem for months and its survival was in a naught.
Then one fine day, it broke the spell of its dormancy.
This lifeless stem sprouted two light green leaves for my
fancy.

Life pops out from the unexpected caverns of stillness.
In a month, the stem wore a crown of green foliage with
blitheness.
Each dawn gives me a reason to rise up and say 'Hello' to
them.
The curry leaves sway in the breeze and recite the
anthem,

Of life full of small happiness, blessings and adulation.
Thank you curry leaves for being my source of
inspiration.

16. I see, I hear, I speak

Eyes
Saw partially.
Ears
Heard half the truth.
Tongue
Blurted unmindfully.
Damage done.
Undoing? Not possible.
Clear glasses reveal clear vision.
Fogged glasses fog the vision.
Clogged ears feed on hearsay.
Listen with a humane heart quietly.
Feel, perceive and speak objectively.

17. The Lighthouse

The Enormous, Titanic ships navigate their course,
Through the ferocious, furious and wild oceans.
The sun guides their path during the day,
But leaves them in the lurch and bids adieu,
To let the night terrify them and let them go astray.

In the darkest hours, the light house standing lonely,
But firm and sturdy, takes charge to guide them quietly.
The Enormous ships proudly trampling and taming the
roaring waters,
Bows down to the light house, for guiding the path, they
have to charter.

Be your own light house, strong and unwavering.
Undeterred by trials, tribulations and uproar,
Guiding the self to navigate the path to your shore.

18. A Promise to Myself

I am going to sail my boat in the rough seas,
And tame the waves as they come to tease.
The odds cannot knock me down,
I will turn them in my favour and wear the crown.

I am not an old, self-contented pond of water,
I am a young rivulet, full of zest, never to falter.
In my struggle to meet the challenges of life.
I am not going to trample others and be a guile.

I am averse to shortcuts for right means justify the ends.
The more you impede my path, the stronger will be my intent.
Alone, I sculpt, chisel and curate my path.
Undeterred by scathing jeering and wrath.

Alone, I enjoy my march with winning spree.
If you raise a hand to point finger at me.
Let the other hand join to clap and cheer for me.